I0457450

PEACEFUL

— PUBLIC —

SPEAKING

Spiritual Meditations to Calm Your
mind before the Big Speech

Rhonda Davis Smith

Quantum
Discovery
A LITERARY AGENC

Peaceful Public Speaking
Copyright © 2023 by Rhonda Davis Smith

All rights reserved. No part of this publication may be reproduced, distributed, or transmitted in any form or by any means, including photocopying, recording, or other electronic or mechanical methods, without the prior written permission of the author, except in the case of brief quotations embodied in critical reviews and certain other non-commercial uses permitted by copyright law.

ISBN
978-1-961601-56-7 (Paperback)
978-1-961601-57-4 (eBook)
978-1-961601-55-0 (Hardcover)

For God hath not given us the spirit of fear,
but of power and of love and of a sound mind.

—*II Timothy 1:7 KJV*

TABLE OF CONTENTS

INTRODUCTION

Imagine this: After a powerful and well-deserved introduction, you walk up to the front of the room, take a deep breath and smile. It is the audience's first indication that they are in the presence of an expert presenter. As you exhale, you survey the crowd and notice that several people are jittery with anticipation. Relaxed and in control, you begin your presentation with a story or joke about the subject, saying a little about yourself. The audience responds easily and appropriately to the emotions you have aroused in them—their second clue that you are a master communicator. Soon they're hanging onto your every word. They trust that what you have to say will improve the quality of their lives. Speaking from your heart, you continue with your message, delivering it exactly as you intended: clearly, confidently, and effectively. At the end, the faces of your listeners assure you that their questions have been answered, that future decision making will be less difficult, or that they are in some way better because of this encounter. Gratified, you step away from the podium and exit to the sound of sustained applause.

Expect nothing less after reading this book.

Delivering a speech before a captivated audience is an experience, I believe you can have each time you are invited to speak. I recognize, however, that because you're reading this book you might be like most people, who would rather do *anything but* stand up and talk before a group of onlookers. As a communications consultant, I've seen firsthand the turmoil that an upcoming speech can cause. So many of those who come to me for help do so because they can't imagine themselves in the above scenario and are terrified of looking incompetent in front of strangers, their friends or colleagues. I wrote this book to help free you from such fears and to challenge you to look at your public speaking opportunities from a different perspective, a spiritual perspective.

Peaceful Public Speaking is a philosophy and set of spiritual laws that are founded on the assurance that the Creator is present and active in every aspect of our lives, including those times when we are called to give a speech in public. The Peaceful Public Speaking ideas set forth here will rid you of pre-speech anxiety and put aside the notion— once and for all—that you must recite the text of your speech over and over again in order to succeed as a presenter. Peaceful Public Speaking will awaken you to the truth that the entire public-speaking process is in God's hands— from the initial invitation to speak, to the composition of the audience, to preparation and development of your presentation, to its actual delivery. In essence, this book views public speaking as an act of service and affirms that you have been invited to speak because you have a special message to deliver to those who will be gathered to hear you.

If that last idea seems a little farfetched to you, I invite you to revisit one of the most well-known figures in the Old Testament of the Bible, the story of Moses. For me, Moses is the quintessential public speaker and I often use his story to illustrate how a willingness to serve can dramatically change our perspective and your ability to deal with the challenges. Here was a man who considered himself totally unqualified to do what God was asking of him, but after he (reluctantly) agreed to accept God's mission for his life, he learned that he possessed exactly what it took to lead the children of Israel out of bondage. That, of course, is why God chose him to do the task. God sees us in our perfection and can use us for great good if we would submit to the urgings of our hearts and focus on our potential instead of our shortcomings. When we do, we discover insights, talents, and synchronicities that can only reveal themselves to us when we are aligned with our divinity. And like Moses, we will be amazed at what we can accomplish and whom we can serve.

Moses' stated objections to doing God's work are equally instructive. Upon closer examination, they reveal the rationale behind the thoughts that result in public-speaking anxiety and show us where our thinking needs to change. Let's look:

MOSES TO GOD: *"But I am not the person for a job like that" Exodus 3:11 KJV*

This is the ego wanting to make an issue of credentials, experience, competence, or lack thereof. For example, you're under the impression that university degrees, impressive certifications, or years of experience, is what qualifies one to give a speech, instead of "why me" a different thought can be "how can I best share what I know about the topic?"

MOSES TO GOD: *"They won't believe me. They won't do what I tell them to" Exodus 4:1 KJV*

Moses, like most of us, believes that it takes "authority" to be a convincing speaker. If he were living today, he would attempt to remedy this lack by doing research and citing the prevailing experts in the field. Under spiritual law, your life experience is your authority, and your most-effective speeches will be built on what you already know to be true.

MOSES TO GOD: Oh Lord, I'm just not a good speaker. I have never been and I am not now…..I have a speech impediment…" Exodus 4:10 KJV

The ego again, this time drawing your attention away from the importance of what you have to say. Set aside any negative thoughts you have about how you will look, or sound giving a speech and consider this: What you think of as a hindrance is often what God uses as a tool for sharing your truth. Say what you have to say from your heart, and you will be, to your audience, as eloquent as the most gifted and charismatic orator.

This book offers a way to correct the above mental errors and to readjust your thoughts and feelings to finally overcome your public speaking anxiety. When you have taken these new ideas to heart and allowed them to sink into your mind, the next time you're asked to give a presentation, you'll do it gladly, authentically, and peacefully.

HOW TO USE THIS BOOK

In the following pages, you will get great ideas to focus on instead of thoughts and ideas that make you feel nervous to give an upcoming presentation. It is important to note that this book is not filled with tips or techniques to become a better speaker; it's filled with thoughts and ideas. Peaceful Public Speaking is a book of thoughts and ideas to help you think of yourself and your message with the confidence and dignity it deserves.

I have been coaching nervous speakers for more than 25 years. The innovative and creative engineers I've spent most of my professional life coaching often feel like a lot is at stake when they give a presentation. Many of the presentations they give are to win multi-million-dollar contracts and the pressure to succeed is intense. Winning a project and the problem-solving innovations that often accompany winning big contracts can elevate their professional status within the company and the industry. It is an oversimplification to say; there is a lot at stake; the company's ability to continue to provide good service to its customers is predicated by the project leader's ability to win the work with a great presentation. To be clear, the part a good presentation plays in winning a big contract is an oversimplification— many things must be in place before we get to the winning presentation.

My role is to bring each speaker to their personal best in the shortest time possible. I've learned it's not a list of do this or do that that relieves the stress; it isn't the direction to act this and say it that way that helps nervous speakers gain confidence. The fastest way to make a nervous speaker better, is to change the mind chatter. It's the voice in your head that says you are not good enough that need to be quieted. If you change the thoughts, you are thinking—and switch to thoughts about how competent you are, how creative, innovative, or how good you are at this task—confidence is almost instantaneous. Think empowering thoughts settles the mind and allows you to focus on giving a great presentation. I've witnessed change happening much faster by shifting the thought. Think empowering thoughts, and your behavior will gladly, easily, and effortlessly change.

Many books will walk you through organizing your thoughts and with tips and techniques to present your ideas. You'll learn how to start with an attention-grabbing introduction and methods to organize the core message, followed by a moving conclusion. Any one of the books on the market today is perfect for helping you draft a speech. After you have done all the necessary and important research and prep, you may still be nervous. Maybe you are lucky enough to have a speech writer or professional draft a speech to deliver; either way, you are still nervous and worried about making a mistake.

This book is the final step in your preparation. Consider this book a coach that gently encourages you with passages that speak to how knowledgeable, smart, and capable you are. The words in this book remind you that you can give a speech, you are worthy, you are ready, and you are the right one to make the presentation. Peaceful Public Speaking is full of inspirational messages to build your confidence as you prepare to give a speech.

I've learned over the years that most are not nervous about the whole idea of giving a speech, not the words on the page, not nervous about the people gathering in the space, or not nervous about the message. Some are nervous about one concept; maybe it's the audience or having to stand up and talk or the message, but not all three. No matter how well written the words are, or how compelling the stories you will tell are, or how much an audience wants to hear what you have to say, you are nervous because you have some thoughts in your head, that have you believing that it's the worst thing you could ever do, give a speech. These thoughts keep reminding you that somehow you are not good enough. I have written this book for those thoughts that keep you feeling small.

In Peaceful Public Speaking, I break down the aspects of a speaking event into three parts: the speaker, the message, and the audience, much like a three-legged stool. When I prepare to coach a person, I identify which leg of the stool is the cause of concern. For a confident speaker, the stool's three legs are sturdy. All three legs of the stool will impact your ability to do a good job when delivering your speech. Like a chair or a table, a wobbly leg can render the furniture unsafe or unstable for use—so too can a wobbly leg on the three-legged public speaking stool–derail a perfectly crafted speech and an eager audience. The secret sauce of this sturdiness is the belief in your ability to deliver the speech and the message in front of the audience. Belief in yourself, confidence in yourself, is the secret sauce. Belief in yourself is an ambiguous concept that is difficult to measure, pin down, and even harder to know when you move from being worried about failing to be ready to do the darn thing.

To ensure we are on the same page, a speaking event can be a situation where you speak behind a podium to an audience, across the table in a conference room at work, or a small gathering of people in a casual setting. A speaking event is where the spotlight is on you for one minute, an hour, or somewhere between. Your speech may be a part of an organized group speaking event, you may sell an item to an individual in an intimate setting, or you may have to give a toast at a wedding or any occasion when you have permission to speak. When others listen, it is a speaking event and is fair game for discussion. To be doubly clear, if you need to organize your thoughts or any other information into a beginning, middle, and end; that's a speech, and if the thought you must give one makes you sick; Peaceful Public Speaking can help will help to quell the angst you feel.

You may be thinking about a speech you must give, but you don't know which leg of the stool has your insides all twisted in a knot. Pull out a piece of paper and write down the three fears that immediately come to mind when you think about having to give a speech in front of an audience. Title the page "Why I don't want to give this speech." Take a minute and write down your concerns. Top three reasons why– at five reasons, stop you over-achiever!! The list you write will help you determine when a section of the book you should start to read first. Your list is the best indication of the area of a speaking event that causes you to have the most self-doubt. What's on your list also indicates where you need more courage to speak your truth.

Peaceful Public Speaking is designed to suggest alternative thoughts to dwell on instead of the thoughts you came to this book with. Thinking about the thoughts in your head is the source of the anxiety. It's an oversimplification to say, think happy thoughts, and you will be fine. Yet, I have seen over and over and over the power that comforting words of wisdom have on a speaker's attitude, disposition, and confidence. The ability to not just change your thoughts but to rest in the feeling that you are worthy, and you are perfectly wise and knowledgeable moves you from feeling nervous incompetence on the inside to acting credible and capable on the outside.

YOU ARE ENOUGH. WE ARE ONE. MY GIFT.

These three simple statements are the cornerstone to your power as a public speaker. They are the key to standing before an audience and giving all, you've got while feeling confident. These statements represent old-soul understandings. Each section heading in Peaceful Public Speaking is a master Spiritual Law. Which means it is the truth for all of humanity. Each subsequent chapter supports and offers proof and a deeper understanding of the sections of Master Law.

The first Master Law, YOU ARE ENOUGH, if you have never heard it said about yourself, can be overwhelming. We don't have to argue about whether I am right or whether you believe those words are True. If you have self-doubt, in the pages of this first section you will find yourself. It is the first leg of the three-legged presentation stool.

As you flip through this book's pages, you notice each of the three sections: has multiple motivational messages. You don't have to read them all; pick one that speaks directly to you. When you identify the passage that resonates, keep reading it and dwelling on it until it takes hold; before long, you'll replace self-doubt with courage.

This may seem off-topic; indulge me, please. When I first began to exercise daily, I didn't want to. I've got a thin frame, I rationalized; I participated in ballet classes from a toddler through high school graduation, and I put in my exercise time. I read this story from a world-famous therapist Marisa Peer; that said, tell yourself something you like or don't like; the mind will do whatever its person tells it to, so I did. I started to say, wherever I saw someone exercise, I like to exercise; when I thought about exercising, I'd say, I like to exercise, and when I started, I would say with excitement, look at me exercising, these exercise clothes are so cute. I don't get an endorphin high from exercising and don't need to lose weight. I exercise because it's good for my long-term health. Same thing for you and your speech; it could be career advancement, sharing a heartfelt message, or a passionate cause.

So why not read a message in the pages of this book and let that thought be the dominant thought you think? Only time will tell; you may be good at speaking, and the audience will love listening to you. Why not think a new thought; what do you have to lose—being scared, self-doubt, fear—you want to hold on to that thought—really?!

Instead, please focus on the chapters in each section; they will help to quiet your mind by giving it empowering ideas to ponder.

If you have self-doubt: read the first section.
Part I I am Enough (The Self)

If you are worried about how the audience will
receive you, read the second section:
Part II We Are One (The Audience)

If you aren't sure your message is the right
message, read the third section:
Part III My Gift (The Message)

Each section begins with some common concerns and worries. Compare the ideas listed to your list of concerns. Comparing the *Peaceful* list of concerns with your own, will help you begin with the section of the book where you will find the most relief. The passages are short, easy to read, and great food for the mind. One or two will speak to you when you find the one that feels like a whisper to your heart, then read and re-read it until it is your dominate thought.

THE SPEAKER'S PRAYER

To the One God that rules both heaven and earth, I stand before you now with a simple request.

Allow me to:

> Easily and effortlessly deliver the words you have placed in my heart. Change my pulsing heartbeat to the rhythm of love.

> Replace my dry throat with a clear loud resonating channel for your word.

> Still my racing mind so that I can focus on delivering a message with clarity and confidence.

> Use my queasy stomach to remind me that I am human. As the messenger, I am no better or worse than the people I stand before.

> Oh Lord, help me to remember one more time…

> Creating a space of mutual love and respect is the key to giving a successful presentation.

PART I

I AM ENOUGH (THE SELF)

o o o o o o o o o o o o o o o o o o o o o o o o o o o o o o o o o o o o o o

And God said, let us make man in our own image, after our likeness: and let them have dominion over the fish of the sea, and over the fowl of the air, and over the cattle, and over all the earth, and over every creeping thing that crept upon the earth. So God created man in his own image, in the image of God created he him; male and female created he them.

—Genesis 1:26-27 KJV

I Am Enough (The Self)

You should be reading the Spiritual Laws in this section if:

- You are a novice presenter
- You spend a lot of time worrying about your self
- Your habit is to continue talking even if your audience seems disinterested
- You are worried that the sale, your reputation, or the good opinion of others rests solely on your presentation
- You suffer from feelings of inadequacy
- You believe you must know every answer to every question, even questions that don't have answers

Or you believe your audience is:

- Preoccupied with speaker's anxiety
- Collectively holding its breath waiting for the speaker to relax
- Not focused on your message, but on you, the speaker
- Too quiet and uninvolved
- Behaving in a way that will disrupt your flow

Or if your message:

- Lacks personal information, anecdotes, or stories
- Overemphasizes outside experts, research, and external data
- Contains little or no opinion or experience

SPIRITUAL LAW#1

Permission Granted

Be still and listen. There is a quiet voice calling your name, asking you to listen. The voice is gently reminding you of the truth. You are enough. What you have to say is perfect. Now is the time. You are anxious because you are looking for an excuse to be little. None are available. You're looking for a reason to back out, not show up as the bright light that you are. Maybe you want to crumble from the weight of obligation. Sorry, not today, your number has been called. It's your time to shine. Tell yourself "I am okay."

You don't need my permission to shine—you have it already—and stop waiting for your boss or co-workers to give you the green light. You also have the permission of your mother, father, grade schoolteacher, and the classmates of your youth. Together we are the chorus of your heart. Stand up and be proud that you have everything it will take to give your upcoming speech.

SPIRITUAL LAW#1

Permission Granted

This little light of mine,
I'm gonna let it shine.
This little light of mine,
I'm gonna let it shine,
This little light of mine,
I'm gonna let it shine.
Let it shine,
Let it shine,
Let it shine.

Written by Larry Dixon Loes

SPIRITUAL LAW#1

—————— • ——————

Permission Granted

Yes! Yes! Yes! Look at yourself in the mirror and say *yes*; I am the one; there is an audience of eager people waiting with anticipation for me to share what I know to be the truth. You can give this speech. You can represent this organization. The shoes of leadership are in your size. Stand up and bathe in the warmth of the bright light of distinction.

It's never too bright—the light is just right. The permission you seek lies within you. You are the right one to give this speech. Say *yes!*

SPIRITUAL LAW#1

Permission Granted

There is no reason to be small, to hold back, or keep quiet about who you are. Know that you can stand before an audience and give them the information they've been longing for. Whenever you speak your truth—whether it is at work, in the community, or the place where you practice your religion—it is an opportunity to do God's work. God is in every audience that gathers, and every topic is a holy one. We're all divinely guided to speak and share everywhere. Remember that anxiety is simply your mind holding back your heart.

SPIRITUAL LAW#2

You Teach to Learn

Have you ever noticed that people who have struggled with a particular dilemma for a long time are usually experts on how to solve it? And why shouldn't they be. They've read all the books, attended every class and seminar on the subject, and watched all the videos! We might know the solutions to all our problems, but we don't always take our own advice. That's why, in a broad sense, every speaker is teaching a message that he or she needs more than anyone in the audience.

The creator has granted us this life for the purpose of learning lessons that will advance our soul's growth. Giving a speech moves us closer to the truth that we are spiritual beings— designed by God—and to learn that we are spiritual beings is ultimately the purpose of all our learning.

SPIRITUAL LAW#2

You Teach to Learn

By the world's standards, speakers are considered experts because it is presumed that they know more about a topic than "ordinary" people, as evidenced by the number of prestigious degrees they hold from prestigious institutions. In the audience's estimation, a speaker becomes an expert when it is evident that he or she struggles with the very problem the audience is attempting to solve. Who do you consider to be the most credible speaker about a particular topic? Whose words resonate in your heart as the truth? Likely, you named someone whose story is similar to your own story. You and that person have walked a mile in the same moccasins. Likewise, your *resonate with* of the issues your audience members are struggling with is what will give you credibility in their eyes.

SPIRITUAL LAW#2

You Teach To Learn

The nervousness you feel preceding a presentation has nothing to do with the content of your speech and everything to do with how willing you are to be healed of your illusions about who you are. You are nervous because your heart is crying out for authenticity but you head is afraid of being "found out." You think it will be obvious to everyone that you don't walk your talk. If you could put aside your insecurities about not having mastered the problems in your life, you could immerse yourself in finding the solutions and, in the process of helping others, help yourself. This is what is truly meant by your "calling" and what will enable you to incorporate the joy, frustration, insight, and mistakes you have gleaned from your life experiences into a powerful and empowering message. The number of engagements on your speaking calendar is a good indicator of how willing you are to meet your personal demons head on and to learn whatever truth the speaking experience has to teach you.

SPIRITUAL LAW#2

You Teach To Learn

You are an expert on your chosen topic, a recognized leader in your field. You know all there is to know; people will sit at your feet eager to hear words from the master.

Nevertheless, you are teaching to learn.

How can that be, you ask? When you speak before an audience, you are teaching others how to stand tall and how to perform well in the light of public scrutiny. You are demonstrating love through disagreement, passion during peril, and confidence in the midst of change.

Once you learn these lessons, you will no longer have to teach them.

SPIRITUAL LAW#3

Action and Their Consequences

We humans get to determine the meaning of each and every event we experience. People who are good at an activity have thoughts that differ from the thoughts of people who believe they are not good at the activity. Consequently, the same activity will have different "meanings" for different people.

What meaning have you given to the act of public speaking? What do you think when you think about speaking in public? What patterns have occurred in your life around public speaking? How are those patterns related to your perceptions about public speaking?

What's the real cause of anxiety about public speaking? It varies with everyone; following are two examples. After proudly delivering her third-grade science report, one of my clients was made the butt of a joke by her teacher. Now, as a professional engineer, every time she makes a speech, someone makes a joke at her expense. Back in high school, a future rocket scientist was laughed at by his classmates because of the way he pronounced certain words. As an adult, he no longer uses those particular words. Instead, he designs his speeches to be understood by the fewest number of people in the audience—his fellow rocket scientists. No one laughs at him now.

What these two people have in common is an incredible amount of anxiety about giving a speech that was set in motion long ago. Similarly, the anxiety you are experiencing now has nothing to do with the content of the speech you are about to deliver, nor is it about the audience. Chances are your first public speaking experience wasn't a good experience and so your mind is preparing you to relive the unpleasantness of that past event. If you want these feelings of inadequacy to go away, go back to the source of the upset and transform your emotions there.

SPIRITUAL LAW#3

Actions and Their Consequences

Many people believe that it's okay to have anxiety about public speaking. "It's normal," they tell themselves and, "It happens to everybody." Don't believe it. *Anxiety about giving a speech is not normal.* It only feels normal because giving a speech has negative connotations in your mind. Your anxiety won't go away, however, until you create a new emotional experience, one that results in a positive, fulfilling public-speaking outcome.

At this moment, it matters little what caused the anxiety you're experiencing; what will make a difference now is how effectively you can learn to diffuse the stress. Can you channel it for good before it turns toxic? Do you want to give public speaking a different meaning for you? The decision is yours to make. You can release the fear, release the negative emotions, and then change the thoughts and feelings about speaking from anxiety to anticipation.

SPIRITUAL LAW#4

The Power of Ahhhhhh!

Your power as a presenter will be totally transformed the moment you stop talking to the people you "see" sitting before you. When you stop dealing with their bad attitudes, rude behavior, and insensitivity to the courage it takes to stand before them, that's the day you will speak as your own true person, sharing your true message. You will never look back.

By the time a speech has ended, very little of its content will be remembered and less than 7%[*] of those in the audience will go back to review their notes. The audience members don't want facts—they want a feeling. By being clear in your mind about the feelings you want to arouse in people, you will be effectively exercising the bit of control you have in the presentation dynamics. Do you want the audience to feel *empowered, excited, informed, motivated,* and *understood?* It's your choice. They may also feel bored, exhausted overwhelmed, undecided, indifferent, turned off. It's up to you.

What will be remembered long after your presentation is not what you said but how you made people feel. The best speakers decide *before the speech* what the feeling will be.

---

[*]   Dr. Albert Mehrabian, UCLA, the 7-35-55 Rule

SPIRITUAL LAW#4

The Power of Ahhhhhh!

Breathing is an excellent way to alleviate the stress of an upcoming speech. To use the breath effectively, simply concentrate on the process of breathing—the expansion and contraction of the lungs—and gently try not to allow your mind to wander. Focus your mind by inhaling through your nose and exhaling through your mouth with an "ahhhhhh." Think of it this way: the inhale frees the mind to receive God's message, and the exhale brings the message from deep within and sends it out to the audience. Practice the three parts of this technique right now:

1. Concentrate only on the inhale and exhale,
   close your eyes if you need to.
2. Breathe in through the nose and with your mouth closed.
3. Breathe out through the mouth and say
   "ahhhhh." The sound of "ahhhhhh" calls the names of God:

   Jehovah
   Allah
   Messiah
   Ra
   Dalai Lama
   Buddha

When you have mastered this technique, people will come up to you after your presentation to tell you how much you've inspired them (yet you will hardly remember what you said). That's how you'll know that God was working through you. By the way, the origin of the word *inspires,* meaning "to breathe," had to do with being under the influence of divine guidance. So breathe, breathe, breathe.

SPIRITUAL LAW#4

The Power of Ah!

God sees only perfection, whereas humans see error. Our challenge is to see as God sees. Imagine yourself knowing the information you need to know to confidently get your point across. But don't get too hung up on "knowledge." Remember that the audience has gathered to hear you speak because they believe you have an important message that will positively affect their lives. Focus on your intention and the passion that wells naturally within you about your subject matter. Look deeply into the eyes of those gathered before you and silently, through your message, tell them they are perfect, they are enough, they are safe. When you do this, the most incredible thing will happen. They'll reflect those sentiments back to you.

SPIRITUAL LAW #4

―――•―――

The Power of Ah!

When your speech is over, you'll want to evaluate yourself. You think it's a good idea to dissect what was good and not so good about it right away. You think this act of comparing how close you stuck to your notes and staging is an indicator of your success as a presenter. It's not. Instead of rushing to critique your performance, simply rest and wait for the only true indicator that your gift has been received:

At least one person will come up to you at some point following your presentation to say thank you.

He or she might also tell you an interesting story about how they came to be part of your audience, or about how much they needed to hear what you had to say. This is a different experience from the feeling you get from a standing ovation or when the whole audience is requesting an encore. That's wonderful, of course, but it's far more gratifying to know that individual lives have been touched by your speech. When someone slips you a note of gratitude or stands in line for hours just to shake your hand, you'll know you were able to serve. There is no better feeling in the world.

PART II

WE ARE ONE (THE AUDIENCE)

o o o o o o o o o o o o o o o o o o o o o o o o o o o o o o o o o o o o o

…When two or more are gathered, in my name, there I am in the midst of them;

—Matthew 18:20 KJV

Be not afraid of their faces; for I am with thee To deliver thee saith the Lord.

—Jeremiah 1:8 KJV

We Are One (The Audience)

You should be reading the Spiritual Laws in this section if you are:

- Preoccupied with the outcome of your presentation (need more business, referrals, applause, contracts, etc.)
- Worried about the audience's opinion
- Interpret the audience's silence as agreement with your message
- Concerned about whether the audience will "like" you and what you have to say

Or if you:

- Appear knowledgeable and confident to others
- Are nervous but mask your anxiety well
- Think it's important to be perceived as an authority or expert
- Take yourself too seriously
- Find it difficult to focus on any one person in the audience

Or if your message:

- Sounds too rehearsed and canned
- Has too much industry language or insider abbreviations
- Focuses on industry facts rather than on your personal experiences
- Lacks personal information, anecdotes, stories, etc.

SPIRITUAL LAW#5

The Holy Audience

The law of compensation, the law of supply and demand, and the law of capitalism all boil down to a simple mathematical equation: One number that is added, subtracted, multiplied, or divided by another number creates a third number. A similar phenomenon occurs in the communication process. When the "vibration" of the sender and the receiver of a message are attuned, they create a new vibration. This combined action is called *synergy*, and it can elevate the energy in a room to unimaginable highs. You can create synergy by giving your audience something to connect to. The best way to do that is by revealing who you are and what you know about the topic of your presentation. Don't be afraid to connect with your audience. When synergy happens during a presentation, transformation occurs for everyone involved.

SPIRITUAL LAW#5

The Holy Audience

It is often assumed that all a good presentation needs is a good presenter; however, the audience is just as important to a great presentation as the speaker is. In fact, you and your audiences are in search of the same satisfaction: acceptance, perfection, and expert status! We know this, which is why speakers struggle with the desire to be approved of in the eyes of an audience (as if it were possible for another to give us a true stamp of approval after a 30-minute presentation).

To receive audience accolades, give them out! This isn't a new concept; what we like in another we desire for our- selves. When a speaker's body language says, "This audience deserves my appreciation," the audience will feel the love inherent in that statement and will do the only logical thing—they'll give it back to the speaker in spades.

SPIRITUAL LAW#5

The Holy Audience

The best lectures are those that give the speaker the opportunity to both teach and learn. Your challenge then is to create a situation that allows you and your audience to be teacher and student. As you're developing your presentation, keep in mind that the audience didn't just arrive by falling off the proverbial turnip truck. They know all kinds of interesting facts and have had many interesting experiences related to your topic. Create an opportunity for them to share their insights with you and you will broaden your own knowledge, which benefit you *and your next audience.*

Think of the presentation you are about to give as though you are riding on a seesaw. When you are lifted in the air, your playmate lands gently on the ground. And vice versa. As the speaker, you get a turn to lift off and speak your truth. Then it's the audience's turn. Allow them to reflect to you the truth they are hearing.

Give and receive. When you are willing to do both, your speech will be on point, your audience will pay more attention, and the clarity you'll each receive will astound you.

SPIRITUAL LAW#6

Give to Receive

One of the most important lessons you'll learn as a public speaker is *not to judge anything or anybody in the speaking situation.* This is also one of the hardest spiritual laws to embrace. When you are standing in the front of the room, you're likely to think that every whisper, every giggle, every side conversation is about you. Rarely is it. Here's how to save yourself the stress that this kind of self- involved paranoia causes:

> *Make it a rule to never make*
> *assumptions about what the audience*
> *is thinking or feeling during your*
> *presentation.*

SPIRITUAL LAW#6

Give to Receive

There is a certain amount of detachment every good speaker practices, and a good time to use it is the moment your mind begins to read the faces of the people gathered as either pleasant faces or trouble-making faces. In some cases, others will try to prepare you for your audience by saying, "this is a tough crowd," or, in a misguided effort to be helpful, they'll report all kinds of other information. Don't get sucked into any preconceived ideas about the crowd—no matter how well-intentioned your informant is. What appears to be a crowd of people in navy blue suits or red dresses is, in truth, a gathering of spiritual bodies hidden behind the appearances of flesh.

Suspend all thoughts of what you think is real and true while you are delivering your speech. Stay in the present moment.

SPIRITUAL LAW#6

Give to Receive

Understand this and you will be a masterful communicator: Your five senses cannot accurately assess the speaking environment. *The function of your senses is not to go out and find the truth but to confirm whatever you believe to be the truth.* In other words, your senses cannot create a reality; they can only validate what you think is a reality. If you are having nervous thoughts, your senses will gather evidence and tell you "You have reason to be nervous." That's why you must learn to speak your truth regardless of what your body might be experiencing.

Talk to the souls in your audience—the part inside of each person that came to your presentation for answers—and then watch yourself give and gain insights with clarity.

SPIRITUAL LAW#7

The Mirror Principle

If you really want to know the depths of your commitment to any cause, stand before a group of people and tell them about it. The audience will reflect your truth as accurately as any mirror. Guaranteed.

SPIRITUAL LAW#7

The Mirror Principle

If you're thinking that you *can't wait to get this over* as you start your speech, that's exactly what the people in the audience will be thinking. If you start your speech thinking *the most incredible information is mine to share,* your audience will think so, too.

The energy of your thoughts affects the audience and is reflected to you. Let the message you send be a confidence- inspiring message. If you want to have the audience sitting on the edge of their seats in anticipation of what you have to say, start by being excited to say it. Think thoughts of joy, trust, fun, learning, peace, expectancy, and excitement. Look at the people seated before you. Look them directly into the eyes. Tell them through your words and the tone of your words that you are worthy and valuable and so are they.

SPIRITUAL LAW #7

The Mirror Principle

The spiritual laws exist whether we believe them or not. Why then, you may wonder, are there terrible audiences? First, let me remind you not to be fooled by the appearance of a "terrible" audience. Audiences reflect to you whatever you think and believe about them, yourself, and your message. They can be challenging in the same way that life is sometimes challenging. One benefit of having a "tough" audience is that the experience drives you to really know your stuff. It's the familiar coal-to-diamond concept. Pressure, chiseling, and polishing transform an elemental substance into a multifaceted and sparkling jewel. Similarly, when you are chiseled and polished by a "tough" crowd, you will delve deeper into your topic and your understanding will rise to the next level, where new insights are possible. You will begin to "get" your own messages.

You are a master when you can declare that "every person who walks into this meeting is supposed to be here. I have a message to give to them, and they have a blessing for me."

SPIRITUAL LAW#8

Questions Are Always Answered

The truth in this law's statement should make it easy to go to sleep at night. You are the answer to any question that might be asked of you as a public speaker. How could you not feel confident in yourself and your abilities with the idea in mind that the audience *needs you* to help them along the path of life? Make this spiritual law the cornerstone to every speech you give and your fears will be calmed by the thought that you can make someone's journey a little easier, make their load a bit lighter, or help to put their problems into perspective.

This spiritual law is the biggest miracle and is the main reason that people are called to speak in public. The universe is ready to answer every question the moment it is asked. You are part of the miracle of an answered prayer. For every event, there is a season; for every question, there is always an answer.

Know it. For no other reason were you called.

SPIRITUAL LAW#8

Questions Are Always Answered

In the book *Conversations with God*, author Neal Donald Walsh writes from God: "Hear Me, everywhere. Whenever you have a question, simply know that I have answered it already. Then open your eyes to your world. My response could be in an article already published. In the sermon already written and about to be delivered. In the movie now being made. In the song just yesterday composed. In the words about to be said by a loved one. In the heart of a new friend about to be made."

In every religion, with every spiritual practice, the seeker is encouraged to seek, approach, and ask. We are promised the synchronicity of an answer. Your message is a vital link in a divine plan and a miracle of timing and coincidence for the people in your audience.

Speak up! You are the gift!

SPIRITUAL LAW#8

Questions Are Always Answered

It's easy to discern when someone has a question that only you can answer. Someone will ask you to speak before an audience.

Simple: test my theory.

Say no to every request to speak for as long as you can. Put up a sign that reads "I'll do anything for you ask except public speaking." After that, if you are still asked to speak before a group,…what's the saying?… "you can run, but you cannot hide."

PART III

MY GIFT (THE MESSAGE)

○ ○

If I had the gift of being able to speak in other languages without learning them and could speak in every language there is in all of heaven and earth but didn't love others, I would only be making noise.

—I Corinthians 13:1
The Living Bible

My Gift (The Message)

You should be reading the Spiritual Laws in this section if your message:

- Was written by someone else
- Is out of your area of expertise
- Is too technical to be engaging
- Is either very detailed or very light on substance
- Lacks humor or opportunities for audience feedback
- Overemphasizes content
- Needs to be read verbatim
- Rarely includes personal experiences

Or if you are:

- Worried that you will be asked questions you cannot answer
- Worried that your peers will judge your speech and that it will reflect well or poorly on you
- Certain others are more qualified to deliver the speech
- Not making prolonged eye contact with members of your audience

Or if you believe your audience:

- Will start to do other work or have side conversations during your speech
- Won't remember much from your speech
- Will ask few questions when called upon

SPIRITUAL LAW#9

Your Life Is Your Message

Many of us erroneously believe that our life experiences don't equal much if we don't have the correct number of academic or professional credentials to list behind our name. There is nothing wrong with having academic degrees, but don't mistake them for validation or credibility. And whatever you do, don't think that without them you cannot do God's work. God knows the purpose and value of all your life experiences and will reveal them to you (and your audiences) in ways that will bring you tremendous joy.

Take stock of your life. I would bet money that your presentation topic is one that excites you and has been an integral part of your life for as long as you can remember.

SPIRITUAL LAW#9

Your Life Is Your Message

We've been taught in the world that facts create opinion. Ask any spin master and he or she will tell you that it is the other way around—opinions shape the facts. Take a scientific approach to preparing your speech: start with a hypothesis—your opinion— and then gather as much material as you choose to substantiate it. What are you waiting for? That's how the experts do it, and this explains why two sides of an argument can be substantiated with the same facts. Each expert uses the research in a way to make it mean what they want it to mean. Research about your topic will validate your ideas or experiences, too, but only after you have agreed to accept your mission.

No matter how passionate you are about your message, there will always be others who disagree with you. That's okay. It's their choice. What's important for you to remember is that the role of the speaker is to serve. You are a servant, not a savior. Depending on what you believe, we've already been "saved," or there's no need for "salvation." Either way, it's not your job.

To serve with your whole heart is one of the highest, noblest callings.

SPIRITUAL LAW#9

Your Life Is Your Message

If you want to deliver a boring lifeless speech like the type often given in company meetings all over the world, I can tell you how. Exclude any mention of personal examples, experiences, or stories. Make sure the entire presentation is based on other people's ideas, particularly people no one has ever heard of. Rattle off facts, statistics, and figures without interpreting them or explaining their significance. I assure you that your audience will consider you a bore.

The reverse is also true. The more you reveal about your personal thoughts and experiences, the more incredibly memorable, life-changing, and crowd-pleasing information will pass through your lips. Guaranteed.

SPIRITUAL LAW#9

Your Life Is Your Message

Are you a messenger healer? Are you one of those people who has spent a considerable amount of time—a couple of years at least— examining your life and changing some of your unfulfilling beliefs? The world is waiting for you. If you're nervous, it's because you are trying to figure out how much of your life to reveal. Don't worry. No one is asking you to be perfect. It's your experiences that are perfect in the truths they reflect. Take the focus off yourself and turn the light on the lessons learned from your journey. Your story is where the audience finds strength. Show them your humanity so that they can accept their own.

SPIRITUAL LAW#10

Intentions Matter

Remember George Bailey, the frustrated businessman played by Jimmy Stewart in the Christmas classic *It's a Wonderful Life*? When George decides it would be better if he'd never been born, he jumps over a bridge to meet his death but instead meets his guardian angel. The angel takes him back through his life and shows him what his town, friends, and family would be like if he had not lived. It is quite a revelation! George sees that in the process of simply living his life he had touched people in ways that were too mind boggling to think about.

The same is true for you. Life is not lived in a vacuum. Each time you get up to make a speech, something happens in someone else's life that may not have occurred if you hadn't spoken your truth.

SPIRITUAL LAW#10

Intentions Matter

When you throw a pebble into the pond, ripples are created. I've sometimes wondered if the size of the rock influences the number of ripples that are generated and how far they expand outward. When you give a speech, *you are the pebble thrown into the pond.* You will absolutely have an impact on the people in the audience and they in turn will pass along your words to others. Your speech could help someone save his job or assist someone else in reducing the stress and confusion in her life. So don't be careless with your words or selfish with your expressions. All the people in the audience and the people in their lives need the influence of your message. Give them the gift they came to receive.

SPIRITUAL LAW#10

Intentions Matter

There is always a question behind the question that your speech seeks to address. When your talk speaks to this "real" question and its answer, you'll connect with your audience instantly. People will tell you that your presentation was so "right on" that they thought you'd been walking around in their heads! They will have difficulty imagining how they were lucky enough to be in the right place at the right time. Let the secret out of the bag: the reason you have such clarity is because you struggle with the same issue. The clearer you are about the mental or emotional message your talk speaks to, the better your chances of creating synergy with the audience and the faster and deeper the synergy will penetrate.

You and your audience need the same truth to heal. When you match your topic with a particular need, you will speak directly to the hearts of your audience.

SPIRITUAL LAW#10

Intentions Matter

You cannot live and not have an impact on someone else's life. Your life changes, shapes, motivates, activates, influences, instructs, helps, shows, sees, teaches, assists, loves, hugs, sets examples for, creates, and touches so many other lives just in the day-to-day process of living. Speak your truth and your living will not go unnoticed.

SPIRITUAL LAW #11

The Message Has No Meaning

The anxiety you are experiencing right now has nothing to do with the speech you are about to deliver. It may seem as though the audience, the material, or your own sense of accomplishment is on trial, but that's not the truth. The anxiety you're feeling isn't about what's going to happen, *it's about what has already occurred.* Your nervousness is based on some forgotten event that giving a speech reminds you of. Remember:

> *You give your message its meaning.*
> It's up to you to decide if you will model confidence and passion about the subject or if you will display worry and concern. It's your choice. The only meaning your message has is the one you give it, and it's a message based on *your opinions, your ideas, and your experiences.*

This speech is another opportunity that life has given you to express who you really are to the world. The real reason you have an audience is because you have something to say. Reveal your insights. What are you waiting for?

SPIRITUAL LAW #11

The Message Has No Meaning

Your message is a gift and the people sitting in the audience are waiting to receive it. The audience needs your message. Allowing them into your world will free them to see more possibilities in their own. It's okay if you don't know how your speech will be received. It's more important for you to present your gift with love and joy than to get caught up in the anxiety of creating the message or the concern of how it will be received. When the giver is excited about the gift, the gift is even more valuable.

The word *communicate,* when broken down into its Latin root, means to "exchange common knowledge, to share a gift."

You want to worry about "what if?" instead, think about the joy you experience when giving someone a present.

SPIRITUAL LAW#11

The Message Has No Meaning

A speech is an opportunity to:
present
deliver
create
give
make
share

with others.

SPIRITUAL LAW#12

Love Is the Power

Scientists haven't given a name to the energy that allows life to replenish itself. Many religions call this energy *God* or *love*. All agree that it has the power to keep the planets aligned and our bodies in sync. You can certainly depend on it to move what's in your heart and mind out of your mouth with eloquence, style, and substance.

SPIRITUAL LAW #12

Love is the Power

Say a prayer toward all four corners of the room where you will deliver your speech. This is one of the ways to make sure love flows from the center outward.

- Bless your speaking space before the audience arrives.

- Bless each person when they walk into your space.

- Bless the words that come from your mouth.

- Bless the receptivity of your message

SPIRITUAL LAW#12

Love is the Power

There is no shortage of love. Give away as much of it as you can. Love is the only thing we need more practice giving.

- Love the folks who ask stupid questions.
- Love the people giggling in a corner of the room.
- Love the people that get up and walk out during your speech.
- Love the folks that try to make you look bad.
- Love the folks who don't understand, won't get it, and don't care.

Train your lips and your mind to say "I love you" over and over and over and over and over.

SPIRITUAL LAW#12

Love is the Power

One thing I know beyond a doubt is that the ability to love yourself and your audience is ultimately the only skill you need to acquire to master public speaking. When you love the audience, however, they come before you; when you can see the healing power of your message and can transcend your own feelings of inadequacy, then you will be able to harness the one power in the universe capable of moving mountains with a single thought.

God bless you now.

ABOUT THE AUTHOR

Rhonda Davis Smith has coached hundreds of people for more than 25 years to confidently present themselves and their message with courage and self-assurance. She has spent more than 20 years working for the world's most trusted infrastructure consulting firm; Rhonda provides public speaking coaching to showcase each speaker's brilliant innovative solutions through sharing a compelling story, for internal and external clients and staff. Smith lives in Washington, DC, with her husband, together they have three adult children.

If you would like to share the ways in which Peaceful Public Speaking has helped you have a more rewarding speaking experience, please write to peacefulpublicspeaking@gmail.com. Thank you.

Allow me to whisper these
kind words to you…

When the time comes, *Stand Tall*
You are Enough

When you hear the audience
applause, *Remember*
We are One

After you research, write,
and prep, *Know*
You are Ready

The world awaits.

www.ingramcontent.com/pod-product-compliance
Lightning Source LLC
Chambersburg PA
CBHW051646120626
46551CB00015B/2237